Mortimer

World's Most Fascinating Guinea Pig

 PUBLISHING

photography by:
{**julie johnson**}

Mortimer Fun Facts:

- He once convinced a vampire bat to become a vegetarian.
- He lives vicariously through himself.
- He once taught a German Shepherd how to bark in Spanish.
- When a tree falls in a forest and no one is there, Mortimer hears it.
- When he is out walking with his owner, roses stop to smell him.
- He has taught many old dogs a variety of new tricks.
- Panhandlers line up to give him money when they see him walking with his owner.
- Batman watches Saturday morning cartoons about Mortimer.
- When his owner takes him to Spain, he chases the bulls while she takes the photos.
- Once, when his owner got pulled over for speeding, Mortimer gave the cop a ticket.

You'll Discover all this and much, much more as you view the world of *Mortimer, The World's Most Fascinating Guinea Pig.*

Mortimer

Copyright © 2018 Photography by Julie Johnson, Vine Images Inc.

Published by KPT Publishing
Minneapolis, Minnesota 55406
www.KPTPublishing.com

ISBN 978-1-944833-35-0

Design and production by Koechel Peterson and Associates, Minneapolis, Minnesota

First printing March 2018

10 9 8 7 6 5 4 3 2 1

Printed in the United States of America

I don't always type <u>backwards</u>.

.siht ekil skool ti,
od I nehw tuB

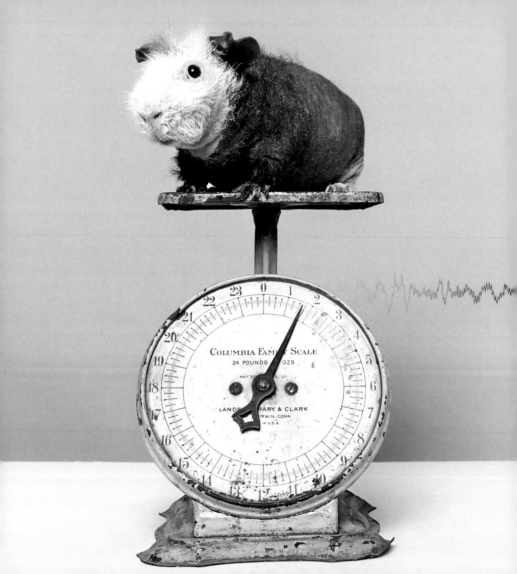

What kind of shape am I in?

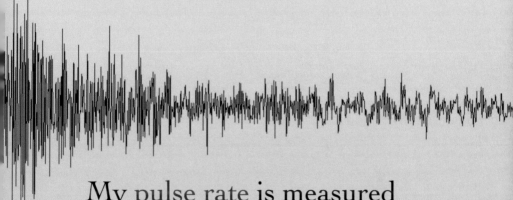

My <u>pulse rate</u> is measured
on the Richter Scale.

I can pick <u>oranges</u>
from an <u>apple</u> tree...

and make the <u>best lemonade</u>
you've ever tasted.

I don't always contradict myself,
but when I do...

I DON'T!

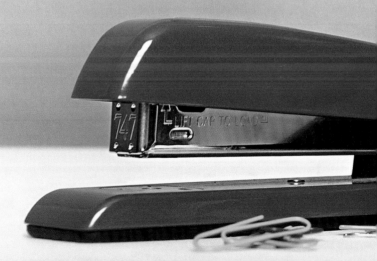

I created the <u>World Wide Web</u>
using a typewriter.

Q: How many licks does it take me to get to the center of a lollipop?

A: Zero. I simply stare at the candy and the outer coating is gone.

I once won a staring contest...

with my <u>own reflection.</u>

HOME *sweet* HOME

When I was a kid I forced my mom to eat her vegetables!

My beard has its own
Social Security number.

When the fire department catches fire...

THEY CALL ME.

Love does not conquer all...

I DO.

<u>Santa</u> writes to me about what he wants for Christmas.

I don't need a <u>license</u> to drive a car...
The car needs a special license
to be driven by me!

Usually when kids go to sleep,
they sleep with a teddy bear...
I sleep with a real bear.

I once climbed the _stairway to heaven,_ and then came back down.

The Guinness Book of World Records
is actually my elementary
school report card.

I can squeeze orange juice
from a <u>banana</u>!

When I play <u>hide-and-seek</u>...
even Google can't find me.

When I swam across the Pacific Ocean, sharks heard the "Jaws" music.

I send my emails through
the <u>postal service</u>!

I once won an underwater
breathing contest with a fish!

I use <u>hot sauce</u> as eye drops!

Love does not conquer all.

I DO!